30 CLASSIC CAKES

Traditional treats for family and friends

SMITHMARK

This edition published in 1996 by
Smithmark Publishers, a division of U.S. Media Holdings Inc.
16 East 32nd Street, New York, NY 10016

Smithmark books are available for bulk purchase and for sales
promotion and for premium use.
For details write or call the Manager of Special Sales, Smithmark
Publishers, 16 East 32nd Street, New York, NY 10016; (212 532-6600)

Produced by
Anness Publishing Limited
1 Boundary Row
London SE1 8HP

Printed and bound in China

10 9 8 7 6 5 4 3 2 1

CONTENTS

INTRODUCTION

Today cake making has rather fallen out of fashion. Our busy life-styles, our attempts at healthy eating and calorie counting and sometimes our lack of baking skills have all contributed to the taste and enjoyment of home-baked goods being banished to just a delightful memory.

One misconception is that making a cake is difficult. This may well have been the case years ago when margarine was hard to cream, sugar may have been lumpy, ovens were unreliable and beating and whisking was laboriously done by hand. Nowadays it really is very easy to whip up a cake in next to no time. Ingredients are prepared, packaged and ready to use and there are mixers and food processors to whisk and blend to perfection in just a few seconds.

The recipes in this book are extremely straight-forward and quick to make. Each finished cake is fully illustrated, with some steps also shown for easy reference.

All of them have been tested and use easy-to-find ingredients and time-saving techniques, so even without any experience you will be able to turn out delicious and stunning cakes that cannot be bought.

There is something irresistible about a home-made cake. The shop-bought variety will never have the same smell, taste or uniqueness. Each time you make a cake it will turn out slightly differently and you can also choose to vary a cake by adding different ingredients or using an alternative shaped cake tin.

It is so much fun to make a cake – be it a simple Carrot Cake for weekend tea with the family to a special cake for Easter or Christmas. Not only will you have fun making the cake, but you will be amazed at how enthusiastically it is received.

So why not bring back those childhood memories of warm freshly baked cake for tea, turn the pages, choose your recipe and enjoy the many rewards that home baking can bring.

LEMON AND APRICOT CAKE

This moreish cake is topped with a crunchy layer of flaked almonds
and pistachios, and is soaked in a tangy lemon syrup after baking
to keep it really moist.

INGREDIENTS

SERVES 10–12
175 g/6 oz/¾ cup butter, softened
175 g/6 oz/1½ cups self-raising flour,
sifted
½ tsp baking powder
175 g/6 oz/¾ cup caster (superfine)
sugar
3 size 3 eggs, lightly beaten
finely grated rind of 1 lemon
175 g/6 oz/1½ cups ready-to-eat dried
apricots, finely chopped
75 g/3 oz/¾ cup ground almonds
40 g/1½ oz/¼ cup pistachios, chopped
50 g/2 oz/½ cup flaked almonds
15 g/½ oz/2 tbsp whole pistachios

FOR THE SYRUP
freshly squeezed juice of 1 lemon
3 tbsp caster (superfine) sugar

STORING
This cake can be kept for up to 3 days
in an airtight container.

1 Preheat the oven to 180°C/350°F/ Gas 4. Grease a 900 g/2 lb loaf tin, line the base and sides with greaseproof (wax) paper and grease the paper. Place the butter, flour and baking powder in a mixing bowl, then add the sugar, eggs and lemon rind. Beat for 1–2 minutes until smooth and glossy and then stir in the apricots, ground almonds and chopped pistachios.

3 To make the lemon syrup, put the lemon juice and sugar into a small saucepan and heat gently, stirring until the sugar has dissolved.

2 Spoon the mixture into the prepared tin and smooth the surface. Sprinkle with the flaked almonds and the whole pistachios. Bake in the centre of the oven for about 1¼ hours, or until a skewer inserted into the centre of the cake comes out clean. Check the cake after about 45 minutes and cover with a piece of foil when the top is nicely brown. Leave the cake to cool in the tin.

4 Spoon the syrup over the cake. When the cake is completely cold, turn it carefully out of the tin and peel off the lining paper.

MARBLED SPICE CAKE

*This cake is baked in a fluted ring-shaped tin called a kugelhopf mould
(Bundt pan) from Germany and Austria to give it a pretty shape.*

INGREDIENTS

SERVES 8–10
75 g/3 oz/6 tbsp butter, softened
*115 g/4 oz/½ cup caster (superfine)
sugar*
2 size 3 eggs, lightly beaten
a few drops of vanilla essence (extract)
*115 g/4 oz/1 cup plain (all-purpose)
flour*
1½ tsp baking powder
3 tbsp milk
3 tbsp black treacle (molasses)
1 tsp mixed spice (apple pie spice)
½ tsp ground ginger
*175 g/6 oz/1½ cups icing
(confectioner's) sugar, sifted, to
decorate*

STORING
*This cake can be kept for up to 2 days
in an airtight container.*

COOK'S TIP
If you do not have a kugelhopf
mould (Bundt pan) or a ring-shaped
cake tin, use a 20 cm/8 inch round
cake tin.

1 Preheat the oven to 180°C/350°F/
Gas 4. Grease and flour a 900 g/
2 lb kugelhopf mould (Bundt pan) or
deep ring-shaped cake tin. Cream the
butter and sugar together in a bowl
until light and fluffy. Beat in the egg
and vanilla essence (extract). Sift
together the flour and baking
powder, then fold into the mixture,
alternating with the milk, until evenly
combined. Spoon about one-third of
the mixture into a small bowl and
stir in the black treacle (molasses)
and spices.

3 Bake in the centre of the oven
for about 50 minutes or until a
skewer inserted into the centre comes
out clean. Leave in the tin for about
10 minutes before turning out on to
a wire rack to cool.

2 Drop alternating spoonfuls of
the light and dark mixtures into
the tin. Run a knife or skewer
through them to give a marbled
effect to the cake.

4 To decorate, stir enough warm
water into the icing
(confectioner's) sugar to make a
smooth icing. Spoon quickly over the
cake. Allow to set before serving.

JEWEL CAKE

*This pretty tea-time cake is excellent served as an afternoon treat
with tea or coffee.*

INGREDIENTS

SERVES 10–15

115 g/4 oz/¾ cup mixed coloured
glacé (candied) cherries, halved,
washed and dried
50 g/2 oz/¼ cup stem (preserved)
ginger in syrup, drained, washed,
dried and chopped
50 g/2 oz/⅓ cup chopped mixed
(candied) peel
115 g/4 oz/1 cup self-raising flour
75 g/3 oz/¾ cup plain (all-purpose)
flour
25 g/1 oz/3 tbsp cornflour (cornstarch)
175 g/6 oz/¾ cup butter
175 g/6 oz/¾ cup caster (superfine)
sugar
3 size 3 eggs
finely grated rind of 1 orange

TO DECORATE

175 g/6 oz/1½ cups icing
(confectioner's) sugar, sifted
2–3 tbsp freshly squeezed orange juice
50 g/2 oz/¼ cup mixed coloured glacé
(candied) cherries, chopped
25 g/1 oz/2½ tbsp chopped mixed
(candied) peel

STORING

*This cake can be kept for up to 2 days
in an airtight container.*

1 Preheat the oven to 180°C/350°F/
Gas 4. Grease a 900 g/2 lb loaf
tin, line the base and sides with
greaseproof (wax) paper and grease
the paper. Place the cherries, ginger
and peel in a plastic bag with 25 g/
1 oz/¼ cup of the self-raising flour
and shake to coat evenly. Sift the
remaining flours and cornflour
(cornstarch) into a small bowl.

2 Place the butter and sugar in a
mixing bowl and beat until light
and fluffy. Beat in the eggs, one at a
time, until evenly blended. Fold in
the flours with the orange rind, then
stir in the fruit. Transfer the cake
mixture to the prepared tin and bake
in the centre of the oven for about
1¼ hours, or until a skewer inserted
into the centre of the cake comes out
clean. Leave the cake in the tin for
5 minutes, then turn out to cool.

3 To decorate the cake, place the
icing (confectioner's) sugar in a
mixing bowl. Stir in the orange juice
and mix until smooth. Drizzle the
icing over the cake. Mix together the
chopped cherries and peel in a small
bowl, then use to decorate the cake.
Allow the icing to set before serving.

SUMMER STRAWBERRY SHORTCAKE

A summer-time treat. Serve with a cool glass of pink sparkling wine
for a truly refreshing dessert.

INGREDIENTS

SERVES 6–8
225 g/8 oz/2 cups plain (all-purpose)
flour
1 tbsp baking powder
½ tsp salt
50 g/2 oz/4 tbsp caster (superfine)
sugar
50 g/2 oz/4 tbsp butter, softened
150 ml/¼ pint/⅔ cup milk
300 ml/½ pint/1¼ cups double (heavy)
cream
450 g/1 lb fresh strawberries, halved
and hulled

STORING
This cake is not suitable for storing.

1 Preheat the oven to 220°C/
425°F/Gas 7. Grease a baking
(cookie) sheet, line with greaseproof
(wax) paper and grease the paper.
Sift the flour, baking powder and salt
together into a large mixing bowl.
Stir in the sugar, cut in the butter
and rub into the flour mixture until
it resembles coarse breadcrumbs. Stir
in just enough milk to make a soft,
pliable dough.

2 Place the dough on a lightly
floured surface and pat into a
30 x 15 cm/12 x 6 inch rectangle.
Cut out two 15 cm/6 inch rounds.
With the back of a knife, mark one
round into eight portions. Place the
rounds on the baking sheet.

3 Bake in the centre of the oven
for 10–15 minutes or until
slightly risen and golden. Leave the
shortcake on the baking sheet for
about 5 minutes, then transfer to a
wire rack, peel off the lining paper
and leave to cool completely.

4 Place the cream in a mixing
bowl and whip until it holds soft
peaks. Place the unmarked shortcake
on a serving plate and spread or pipe
with half of the cream. Top with
two-thirds of the strawberries, then
the other shortcake. Use the
remaining cream and strawberries to
decorate the top layer. Chill for at
least 30 minutes before serving.

CARROT CAKE

*So easy to make, this is a wonderfully moist and tasty cake, enriched
with grated carrots and vegetable oil – a classic "all-in-one" cake.*

INGREDIENTS

SERVES 8

*225 g/8 oz/1 cup caster (superfine)
sugar*
3 size 3 eggs
*200 ml/7 fl oz/scant 1 cup
vegetable oil*
grated rind and juice of 1 orange
*225 g/8 oz/2 cups self-raising
wholemeal (whole wheat) flour*
1 tsp ground cinnamon
½ tsp grated nutmeg
½ tsp salt
*350 g/12 oz/2½ cups grated carrot,
squeezed dry*
115 g/4 oz/1 cup walnuts, ground
225 g/8 oz/1 cup cream cheese
2 tbsp clear honey
1 tbsp orange juice

TO DECORATE

*50 g/2 oz/¼ cup ready-made marzipan
orange food colouring
angelica
2 walnut halves (optional)*

STORING

*This cake keeps for up to 1 week in an
airtight container.*

1 Preheat the oven to 180°C/350°F/
Gas 4. Lightly grease a deep
20 cm/8 inch round cake tin, line
with greaseproof (wax) paper and
grease the paper. Beat the sugar,
eggs, oil, orange rind and juice
together until light and frothy. Sift in
the flour, spices and salt and beat for
1 minute. Stir in the carrots and nuts
and transfer to the tin. Bake for
1½– 1¾ hours or until a skewer
inserted into the centre comes out
clean. Leave in the tin for 10 minutes
before turning out on to a wire rack.

3 Tint the marzipan with the food
colouring to resemble the colour
of carrots.

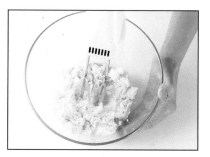

2 To make the icing, beat the
cheese, honey and 1 tbsp orange
juice together until smooth. Chill for
30 minutes until firm.

4 Break off small pieces and roll
between your palms to form
carrot shapes. Using a small knife,
press marks around the sides and
stick a small piece of angelica in the
top of each one for the stalk. Spread
the icing over the top of the cooled
cake. Arrange the carrots in the
centre of the cake and decorate with
the walnut halves, if using.

BANANA COCONUT CAKE

Slightly over-ripe bananas are best for this perfect coffee morning cake.

INGREDIENTS

SERVES 8–10
*75 g/3 oz/1½ cups desiccated
(shredded) coconut*
115 g/4 oz/½ cup butter, softened
*115 g/4 oz/½ cup caster (superfine)
sugar*
2 size 3 eggs
115 g/4 oz/1 cup self-raising flour
*50 g/2 oz/½ cup plain (all-purpose)
flour*
*1 tsp bicarbonate of soda
(baking soda)*
120 ml/4 fl oz/½ cup milk
2 large bananas, peeled and mashed

FOR THE TOPPING
25 g/1 oz/2 tbsp butter
2 tbsp clear honey
*115 g/4 oz/2 cups desiccated
(shredded) coconut*

STORING
*This cake will keep for up to 2 days in
an airtight container.*

3 Bake in the centre of the oven
for about 1 hour, or until a
skewer inserted into the centre of the
cake comes out clean. Leave the cake
in the tin for about 5 minutes, then
turn out on to a wire rack, peel
off the lining paper and leave to
cool completely.

1 Preheat the oven to 190°C/375°F/
Gas 5. Grease a deep 18 cm/
7 inch square cake tin, line the base
and sides with greaseproof (wax)
paper and then grease the paper.
Spread the coconut out on a baking
(cookie) sheet and place under a hot
grill (broiler) for about 5 minutes,
stirring and turning the coconut until
evenly toasted.

2 Place the softened butter and
caster (superfine) sugar in a
mixing bowl and beat until they are
smooth and creamy. Beat in the eggs,
one at a time. Sift together the self-
raising and plain (all-purpose) flours
and bicarbonate of soda (baking
soda), then sift half of this mixture
into the butter and egg mixture and
stir to mix. Mix together the milk
and mashed banana in a small bowl,
then add half to the egg mixture.
Beat well to combine. Add the
remaining flour and toasted coconut
together with the remaining banana
mixture. Stir to mix. Spoon the
mixture into the prepared cake tin
and smooth the surface with a
wet knife.

4 To make the topping, place the
butter and honey in a small
saucepan and heat gently until melted.
Stir in the desiccated (shredded)
coconut and cook, stirring constantly,
for about 5 minutes or until lightly
browned. Remove from the heat and
allow to cool slightly. Spoon the
topping over the top of the cake
and allow to cool completely
before serving.

CRUNCHY-TOPPED MADEIRA CAKE

Traditionally served with a glass of Madeira wine in Victorian England,
this light sponge still makes a perfect tea-time treat.

INGREDIENTS

SERVES 8–10
200 g/7 oz/scant 1 cup butter, softened
finely grated rind of 1 lemon
150 g/5 oz/¾ cup caster (superfine)
sugar
3 size 3 eggs
75 g/3 oz/¾ cup plain (all-purpose)
flour, sifted
150 g/5 oz/1¼ cups self-raising flour,
sifted

FOR THE TOPPING
3 tbsp clear honey
115 g/4 oz/¾ cup plus 2 tbsp chopped
mixed (candied) peel
50 g/2 oz/½ cup flaked almonds

STORING
This cake can be kept for up to 3 days
in an airtight container.

1 Preheat the oven to 180°C/350°F/ Gas 4. Grease a 450 g/1 lb loaf tin, line the base and sides with greaseproof (wax) paper and grease the paper. Place the butter, lemon rind and sugar in a mixing bowl and beat until light and fluffy. Beat in the eggs, one at a time, beating well after each addition until evenly blended.

2 Sift together the flours, then stir into the egg mixture. Transfer the cake mixture to the prepared tin and smooth the surface. Bake in the centre of the oven for 45–50 minutes or until a skewer inserted into the centre of the cake comes out clean. Leave the cake in the tin for about 5 minutes. Turn out on to a wire rack, peel off the lining paper and leave to cool completely.

3 To make the topping, place the honey, chopped mixed (candied) peel and flaked almonds in a small saucepan and heat gently until the honey melts. Remove from the heat and stir briefly to coat the peel and almonds, then spread over the top of the cake. Allow to cool completely before serving.

GORGEOUS CHOCOLATE CAKE

This recipe will definitely make you famous. Make sure you serve it with
paper and pen, as everyone will want to take down the recipe.

INGREDIENTS

SERVES 8–10
175 g/6 oz/¾ cup butter, softened
115 g/4 oz/½ cup caster (superfine)
sugar
250 g/9 oz plain (semi-sweet)
chocolate, melted
200 g/7 oz/2 cups ground almonds
4 size 3 eggs, separated
115 g/4 oz white chocolate, melted,
to decorate

STORING
This cake can be kept for up to 4 days
in an airtight container.

COOK'S TIP
To make the chocolate leaves, wash
5 or 6 rose leaves well and dry on
kitchen paper (paper towels). Brush
the underside of each leaf with the
melted white chocolate. Place the
leaves chocolate-side up on non-stick
baking paper (baking parchment),
and leave to set in a cool place. Peel
the leaf from the chocolate and use
as required.

1 Preheat the oven to 180°C/350°F/
Gas 4. Grease a deep 21 cm/
8 inch springform cake tin, then line
the base with greaseproof (wax)
paper and grease the paper. Place
115 g/4 oz/½ cup of the butter and
all the sugar in a mixing bowl and
beat until light and fluffy. Add two-
thirds of the plain (semi-sweet)
chocolate, the ground almonds and
the egg yolks and beat until they are
evenly blended.

2 Whisk the egg whites in another
clean, dry bowl until stiff. Fold
them into the chocolate mixture, then
transfer to the prepared tin and
smooth the surface. Bake for 50–55
minutes or until a skewer inserted
into the centre of the cake comes out
clean. Leave the cake in the tin for
about 5 minutes, then turn out on to
a wire rack, peel off the lining paper
and leave to cool completely.

3 Place the remaining butter and
remaining melted plain chocolate
in a saucepan. Heat very gently,
stirring constantly, until melted. Pour
over the cake, allowing the topping
to coat the sides. Leave to set for at
least an hour. To decorate, fill a
piping bag with the melted white
chocolate and snip the end. Drizzle
all around the edges to make a
double border. Use any remaining
chocolate to make leaves.

APPLE CRUMBLE CAKE

In the autumn use windfall apples. Served warm with double (heavy) cream
or custard this cake doubles as a marvellous dessert.

INGREDIENTS

SERVES 8–10
75 g/3 oz/¾ cup self-raising flour
½ tsp ground cinnamon
40 g/1½ oz/3 tbsp butter
25 g/1 oz/2 tbsp caster (superfine)
sugar

FOR THE BASE
50 g/2 oz/4 tbsp butter, softened
75 g/3 oz/6 tbsp caster (superfine)
sugar
1 size 3 egg, beaten
115 g/4 oz/1 cup self-raising flour,
sifted
cooking apples, peeled,
cored and sliced
50 g/2 oz/½ cup sultanas
(golden raisins)

TO DECORATE
1 red eating apple, cored, thinly sliced
and tossed in lemon juice
2 tbsp caster (superfine) sugar
pinch of ground cinnamon

1 Preheat the oven to 180°C/350°F/
Gas 4. Grease a deep 18 cm/
7 inch springform tin, line with
greaseproof (wax) paper and grease
the paper. To make the topping, sift
the flour and cinnamon into a mixing
bowl. Rub the butter into the flour
until it resembles breadcrumbs, then
stir in the sugar. Set aside.

2 To make the base, put the
butter, sugar, egg and flour into
a bowl and beat for 1–2 minutes
until smooth. Spoon into the
prepared tin. Mix together the apple
slices and sultanas (golden raisins)
and spread them over the top.

3 Sprinkle with the topping. Bake
in the centre of the oven for
about 1 hour. Cool in the tin for
10 minutes before turning out on to
a wire rack and peeling off the lining
paper. Serve warm or cool, decorated
with slices of red eating apple and
with the sugar and cinnamon
sprinkled over.

UPSIDE-DOWN PEAR & GINGER CAKE

A light spicy sponge topped with glossy baked fruit and ginger. This is also good served warm for pudding.

INGREDIENTS

SERVES 6–8
900 g/2 lb can pear halves, drained
8 tbsp finely chopped stem (preserved)
ginger
8 tbsp ginger syrup from
the jar
175 g/6 oz/1½ cups self-raising flour
½ tsp baking powder
1 tsp ground ginger
175 g/6 oz/¾ cup soft light brown
sugar
175 g/6 oz/¾ cup butter, softened
3 size 3 eggs, lightly beaten

1 Preheat the oven to 180°C/350°F/ Gas 4. Grease a deep 20 cm/ 8 inch round cake tin, line with greaseproof (wax) paper and grease the paper. Fill the pears with half the chopped ginger. Arrange the pears, flat sides down, in the tin. Spoon half the ginger syrup over the top.

2 Sift the flour, baking powder and ground ginger into a mixing bowl. Stir in the soft brown sugar and butter, then add the eggs and beat together for 1–2 minutes until light and creamy. Spoon the mixture into the tin and smooth the surface.

3 Bake in the centre of the oven for 50 minutes, or until a skewer inserted in the centre of the cake comes out clean. Leave the cake in the tin for 5 minutes. Then turn out and leave to cool. Add the reserved chopped ginger to the pear halves and drizzle over the remaining ginger syrup.

SOUR CREAM CRUMBLE CAKE

A deliciously moist sponge, filled and topped with a spicy crumble of walnuts, brown sugar and cinnamon. For a special treat serve with whipped cream or Greek-style yogurt.

INGREDIENTS

SERVES 12–14
115 g/4 oz/½ cup butter,
at room temperature
125 g/4½ oz/¾ cup caster (superfine)
sugar
3 size 3 eggs, at room temperature
215 g/7½ oz/scant 2 cups plain
(all-purpose) flour
1 tsp bicarbonate of soda
(baking soda)
1 tsp baking powder
250 ml/8 fl oz/1 cup sour cream

FOR THE TOPPING
225 g/8 oz/1½ cups dark brown sugar
2 tsp ground cinnamon
115 g/4 oz/1 cup walnuts,
finely chopped
50 g/2 oz/¼ cup cold butter,
cut into pieces

STORING
This cake can be kept for up to 3 days in an airtight container.

1 Preheat the oven to 180°C/350°F/ Gas 4. Grease a deep 23 cm/ 9 inch square cake tin then line the base with greaseproof (wax) paper and grease the paper. For the topping, place the brown sugar, cinnamon and walnuts in a bowl. Rub together with your fingertips, then rub in the butter and continue working until the mixture resembles breadcrumbs.

2 To make the cake, cream the butter until soft. Add the sugar and continue beating until the mixture is light and fluffy. Add the eggs, one at a time, beating well after each addition.

3 In another bowl, sift the flour, bicarbonate of soda (baking soda) and baking powder together three times. Fold the dry ingredients into the butter mixture in 3 batches, alternating with the sour cream. Fold in each addition until well-blended.

4 Pour half of the batter into the prepared tin and sprinkle over half of the walnut crumb topping mixture. Pour the remaining batter on top and sprinkle over the remaining walnut crumb mixture. Bake until brown, 60–70 minutes. Let the cake stand for 5 minutes, then turn it out to cool on a rack.

PEAR AND CARDAMOM SPICE CAKE

Fresh pear and cardamom – a classic combination of flavours – are used together in this moist fruit and nut cake to provide a delicious, mouthwatering tea-time treat.

INGREDIENTS

SERVES 8–12
115 g/4 oz/½ cup butter
115 g/4 oz/½ cup caster (superfine) sugar
2 size 3 eggs, lightly beaten
225 g/8 oz/2 cups plain (all-purpose) flour
1 tbsp baking powder
2 tbsp milk
crushed seeds from 2 cardamom pods
50 g/2 oz/½ cup walnuts, chopped
1 tbsp poppy seeds
575 g/1¼ lb dessert pears, peeled, cored and thinly sliced

FOR THE TOPPING
3 walnut halves
reserved pear slices
3 tbsp clear honey

STORING
This cake can be kept in an airtight container for several days.

1 Preheat the oven to 180°C/350°F/Gas 4. Lightly grease a deep 20 cm/8 inch round loose-based cake tin, line the base with greaseproof (wax) paper and grease the paper. Cream the butter and caster (superfine) sugar together until the mixture is light and fluffy. Gradually beat in the eggs, a little at a time, until evenly blended. Sift the plain (all-purpose) flour and baking powder together, and then fold in gradually along with the milk.

3 Place the 3 walnut halves in the the centre of the cake mixture, and fan the reserved pear slices around the walnuts, covering the cake mixture. Bake for 1¼–1½ hours, or until a skewer inserted into the centre comes out clean.

2 Stir in the cardamom seeds, chopped nuts and poppy seeds. Reserve one-third of the pear slices; chop the rest. Fold the chopped pears into the creamed mixture. Transfer to the prepared tin. Smooth the surface, making a small dip in the centre.

4 Remove the cake from the oven and brush with the clear honey. Cool in the tin for 20 minutes, and then transfer to a wire rack and allow to cool completely.

DUNDEE CAKE

*This is the perfect fruit cake for those who prefer a lighter-style cake. It has
a wonderful fruit and nut flavour and a light, slightly crumbly texture.*

INGREDIENTS

SERVES 16–20
175 g/6 oz/¾ cup butter
176 g/6 oz/scant ¾ cup light soft
brown sugar
3 size 3 eggs
225 g/8 oz/2 cups plain (all-purpose)
flour
2 tsp baking powder
1 tsp ground cinnamon
½ tsp ground cloves
¼ tsp ground nutmeg
225 g/8 oz/1¼ cups sultanas
(golden raisins)
175 g/6 oz/1 cup raisins
175 g/6 oz/1 cup glacé (candied)
cherries, halved
115 g/4 oz/¾ cup chopped mixed
(candied) peel
50 g/2 oz/¾ cup blanched almonds,
chopped
grated rind 1 lemon
2 tbsp brandy

FOR THE TOPPING
75–115 g/3–4 oz/¾–1cup whole
blanched almonds

STORING
*All fruit cakes improve in flavour if
left in a cool place for up to three
months. Wrap the cake in a double
layer of foil.*

2 Spoon into the prepared tin,
smooth the surface, making a
small dip in the centre.

1 Preheat the oven to 160°C/325°F/
Gas 3. Grease a deep 20 cm/
8 inch round cake tin, line the base
and sides with greaseproof (wax)
paper and then grease the paper.
Cream the butter and sugar together
until light and fluffy. Add the eggs,
one at a time, beating well after each
addition. Sift the flour, baking
powder and spices together and fold
into the creamed mixture alternately
with the remaining ingredients, until
evenly incorporated.

3 Decorate the top of the cake
mixture by pressing the almonds
in decreasing circles over the entire
surface. Bake for 2–2¼ hours, or
until a skewer inserted in the centre
comes out clean. Remove from the
oven, cool in the tin for 30 minutes,
and then transfer to a wire rack to
cool completely.

ALMOND AND APRICOT CAKE

Although canned apricots can be used in this recipe, nothing quite beats using the fresh fruit in season. Choose sweet-smelling, ripe fruit for this delicious cake.

INGREDIENTS

SERVES 6–8

4–5 tbsp fine dry white breadcrumbs
225 g/8 oz/1 cup butter, softened
225 g/8 oz/1 cup caster (superfine) sugar
4 size 3 eggs
175 g/6 oz/1½ cups self-raising flour, sifted
1–2 tbsp milk
115 g/4 oz/1 cup ground almonds
a few drops of almond essence (extract)
450 g/1 lb fresh apricots, stoned (pitted) and halved
sifted caster (superfine) sugar, to decorate

STORING

This cake can be kept for up to 3 days in an airtight container.

1 Preheat the oven to 180°C/350°F/ Gas 4. Grease a 23 cm/9 inch round cake tin, line the base with greaseproof (wax) paper and grease the paper. Sprinkle the breadcrumbs into the prepared cake tin and tap them around the tin to coat the base and sides evenly.

2 Place the butter and sugar in a mixing bowl and beat until light and fluffy. Beat in the eggs, one at a time, then fold in the flour, together with the milk, ground almonds and almond essence (extract).

3 Spoon half of the cake mixture into the prepared tin and smooth the surface. Arrange half of the apricots over the top, then spoon over the remaining cake mixture. Finish with the other half of the apricots. Bake the cake in the centre of the oven for 30–35 minutes, or until a skewer inserted into the centre of the cake comes out clean. Turn the cake out on to a wire rack, peel off the lining paper and sprinkle over the sifted caster (superfine) sugar. Serve warm or leave to cool.

MISSISSIPPI MUD CAKE

*This dark cocoa-based chocolate cake is meant to be reminiscent
of the cocoa-black shores of the Mississippi River.*

INGREDIENTS

SERVES 8–10
unsweetened cocoa powder
275 g/10 oz/2½ cups plain
(all-purpose) flour
1 tsp baking powder
150 g/5 oz unsweetened chocolate
225 g/8 oz/1 cup unsalted (sweet)
butter
300 ml/½ pint/1¼ cups strong coffee
pinch of salt
400 g/14 oz/2 cups granulated sugar
60 ml/2 fl oz/¼ cup whisky
2 size 3 eggs, lightly beaten
2 tsp vanilla essence (extract)
115 g/4 oz/1 cup sweetened desiccated
(shredded) coconut

FOR THE FILLING

250 ml/8 fl oz/1 cup evaporated milk
115 g/4 oz/⅔ cup light brown sugar
115 g/4 oz/½ cup unsalted (sweet)
butter
75 g/3 oz plain (semi-sweet) chocolate
3 egg yolks, lightly beaten
1 tsp vanilla essence (extract)
225 g/8 oz/2 cups pecan nuts, chopped
70 g/2½ oz/1 cup miniature
marshmallows

FOR THE TOPPING

350 ml/12 fl oz/1½ cups whipping or
double (heavy) cream
1 tsp vanilla essence (extract)
coconut ruffles (see step 4)

1 Preheat the oven to 180°C/350°F/
Gas 4. Grease 2 x 23 cm/9 inch
cake tins and dust the bases and sides
with cocoa powder. In a bowl sift the
flour and baking powder. In
a saucepan over a low heat, melt the
chocolate, butter, coffee, salt and
sugar, stirring occasionally until the
sugar has dissolved. Stir in the
whisky. Pour the chocolate mixture
into a bowl and cool. Beat in the
eggs and vanilla. Stir in the flour and
coconut. Pour into the prepared tins,
then bake for 25–30 minutes or until
a skewer inserted in the centre comes
out clean. Cool in the tins on a wire
rack for 10 minutes, then turn out
on to the wire rack and leave to
cool completely.

2 For the filling, put the
evaporated milk, sugar, butter,
chocolate, egg yolks and vanilla in a
saucepan. Cook over a medium heat,
stirring frequently for 8–10 minutes
until the chocolate has melted and
the mixture coats the back of a
wooden spoon; do not boil or the
mixture will curdle. Remove from
the heat and add the nuts and
marshmallows, stirring until melted.
Chill until thick enough to spread,
stirring occasionally.

3 Slice both cake layers in half horizontally. Spread each of the bottom cake layers with half the chocolate nut filling and top with the other halves. Whip the cream and the vanilla until it holds firm peaks. Place one filled cake on a plate and spread with half the whipped cream. Top with the second filled cake and spread with the remaining cream.

4 To make the coconut ruffles, puncture the eyes of a coconut with a nail and hammer. Drain, then crack the coconut open using the hammer. Remove the flesh from the shell using a strong, blunt-bladed knife. Rinse in cold water. Using a potato peeler, shave along the curved edge of a coconut piece to give thin wide curls with a brown edge. Use to decorate the cake.

CHILLED GRAPE CHEESECAKE

An attractive and unusual topping decorates this classic chilled cheesecake.
Use green grapes and white grape juice if wished, for an equally attractive cheesecake.

INGREDIENTS

SERVES 12
175 g/6 oz/2 cups crushed gingernuts
(ginger cookies)
50 g/2 oz/¼ cup unsalted (sweet)
butter, melted
350 g/12 oz/1½ cups cream cheese
200 g/7 oz/1 scant cup fromage frais
6 tbsp clear honey
2 size 3 eggs, separated
1 tsp grated lemon rind
1 tbsp lemon juice
4 tbsp Muscat de Beaumes
de Venise (or other sweet white
dessert wine)
1 tbsp powdered gelatine

FOR THE TOPPING
115 g/4 oz red or green seedless
grapes, halved
small piece angelica
2 tbsp Muscat de Beaumes
de Venise (or other sweet white
dessert wine)
1½ tsp powdered gelatine
300 ml/½ pt/1¼ cups red or white
grape juice

STORING
Place in an airtight container and keep
in the refrigerator for up to 3 days.

1 Grease a 23 cm/9 inch round springform tin and line the sides with non-stick baking paper (baking parchment). Combine the gingernuts (ginger cookies) with the butter until well mixed. Press into the base of the prepared tin. Smooth the surface with a metal spoon and chill for 20 minutes. To prepare the cake mixture, beat the cheese, fromage frais, honey, egg yolks, lemon rind and juice in a bowl, until smooth and creamy.

3 When the cheesecake is just setting, remove from the refrigerator and arrange the grapes over the top, in the shape of a bunch of grapes, and make a stalk from the angelica. Chill until completely set. For the topping, heat the 2 tbsp of wine and the gelatine together as before, until dissolved. Pour in the grape juice and leave to go cold.

2 Heat the 4 tbsp of wine and the gelatine together in a small pan, over a low heat, until the gelatine dissolves. Remove from the heat, stir in a little of the creamed mixture, and pour back into the remaining creamed mixture mixing until combined. Whisk the egg whites until stiff and fold thoroughly into the creamed mixture. Pour over the chilled biscuit (cookie) base and chill.

4 Using a small paintbrush, carefully dampen the edges of the lined tin, directly above the set cheesecake. Carefully pour over the cooled grape juice to cover the grapes and chill until set. Just before serving, remove the tin from the side of the cheesecake and carefully peel away the lining paper using a palette knife (metal spatula) to help.

RASPBERRY-HAZELNUT MERINGUE CAKE

*Crisp layers of hazelnut meringue, whipped cream and fresh raspberries make this a
wonderful dessert to serve at a summer dinner party.*

INGREDIENTS

SERVES 8
150 g/5 oz/1¼ cups shelled hazelnuts
4 egg whites
¼ tsp salt
*200 g/7 oz/1 cup caster (superfine)
sugar*
½ tsp vanilla essence (extract)

FOR THE FILLING
*300 ml/½ pint/1¼ cups whipping
cream*
700 g/1½ lb/4 cups raspberries

STORING
This cake is not suitable for storing.

1 Preheat the oven to 180°C/350°F/
Gas 4. Grease two 20 cm/8 inch
sandwich tins and line the bases with
greaseproof (wax) paper, and grease
the paper. Spread the hazelnuts on a
baking (cookie) sheet and bake until
lightly toasted, about 8 minutes.
Leave the nuts to cool slightly.

2 Rub the hazelnuts in a clean
dish towel to remove the skins.
Grind the nuts in a food processor or
coffee grinder until they are the
consistency of coarse sand. Reduce
the oven to 150°C/300°F/Gas 2.

3 With an electric mixer, beat the
egg whites and salt until they
hold stiff peaks. Beat in 2 tbsp of the
sugar, then fold in the remaining
sugar, a few tablespoons at a time.
Fold in the vanilla essence (extract)
and the ground hazelnuts.

4 Divide the batter between the
prepared tins and spread level.
Bake in the oven for 1¼ hours. If the
meringues brown too quickly, protect
with a sheet of foil. Leave to stand
for 5 minutes, then carefully run a
palette knife (metal spatula) around
the inside edge of the tins to loosen.
Turn out on to a wire rack to cool.

5 For the filling, whip the cream
until firm. Spread half the cream
on one meringue and top with half
the raspberries. Top with the other
meringue. Spread the remaining
cream on top and decorate with the
remaining raspberries. Chill for about
1 hour to make cutting easier.

Black Forest Gateau

A perfect gâteau for a special occasion tea party, or for serving as a sumptuous dessert at a dinner party.

Ingredients

Serves 10–12
5 size 3 eggs
175 g/6 oz/¾ cup caster
(superfine) sugar
50 g/2 oz/½ cup plain (all-purpose)
flour, sifted
50 g/2 oz/¼ cup cocoa powder, sifted
75 g/3 oz/6 tbsp butter, melted

For the Filling
5–6 tbsp Kirsch
600 ml/1 pint/2½ cups double
(heavy) cream
425 g/15 oz can black cherries,
drained, stoned (pitted) and chopped

To Decorate
225 g/8 oz plain
(semi-sweet) chocolate
15–20 fresh cherries, preferably
with stems
sifted icing (confectioner's) sugar
(optional)

1 Preheat the oven to 180°C/ 350°F/Gas 4. Carefully grease two deep 20 cm/8 inch round cake tins, line both of the bases with greaseproof (wax) paper and then lightly grease the paper. Place the eggs and caster (superfine) sugar in a large mixing bowl and beat with an electric mixer for about 10 minutes or until the mixture is thick and pale in colour.

3 Cut each cake horizontally in half and sprinkle with the Kirsch. In a large bowl, whip the cream until it holds soft peaks. Transfer two-thirds of the cream to another bowl and stir in the chopped cherries. Place a layer of cake on a plate and spread over one-third of the filling. Top with another layer of cake and continue layering, finishing with a layer of cake. Use the remaining whipped cream to cover the top and sides of the gâteau.

2 Sift together the plain (all-purpose) flour and cocoa powder, then sift again into the whisked egg mixture. Fold in very gently to retain as much air as possible, then slowly trickle in the melted butter and fold in gently. Carefully divide the mixture between the prepared tins. Bake in the centre of the oven for about 30 minutes, or until the tops of the cakes are springy to the touch. Leave in the tins for about 5 minutes, then turn out on to a wire rack, peel off the lining paper and leave the cakes to cool completely.

4 To decorate the gâteau, melt the chocolate in a bowl over a pan of hot water. Spread the chocolate out on to a plastic chopping board and allow to set. Using a long sharp knife, scrape along the surface of the chocolate to make thin shavings and use these to cover the sides and the top of the cake. Arrange the cherries on top of the gâteau. Dust with icing (confectioner's) sugar, if wished.

LUXURY WHITE CHOCOLATE CHEESECAKE

To ensure an even crust, use a dessertspoon or tablespoon to press the crumbs on to the base and side of the tin.

INGREDIENTS

SERVES 16–20
150 g/5 oz (about 16–18) digestive biscuits (graham crackers)
70 g/2½ oz/generous ½ cup blanched hazelnuts, toasted
50 g/2 oz/4 tbsp unsalted (sweet) butter, melted
½ tsp ground cinnamon

FOR THE FILLING
350 g/12 oz fine quality white chocolate, chopped
120 ml/4 fl oz/½ cup whipping or double (heavy) cream
675 g/1½ lb/3 cups cream cheese, softened
50 g/2 oz/¼ cup granulated sugar
4 size 3 eggs
2 tbsp hazelnut-flavour liqueur or 1 tbsp vanilla essence (extract)

FOR THE TOPPING
425 ml/15 fl oz/1¼ cups sour cream
50 g/2 oz/¼ cup granulated sugar
1 tbsp hazelnut-flavour liqueur or 1 tsp vanilla essence (extract)
white chocolate curls to decorate
cocoa powder for dusting (optional)

STORING
Place in a covered container and keep in the refrigerator for up to 2 days.

1 Preheat the oven to 180°C/350°F/ Gas 4. Then carefully grease a 23 cm/9 inch springform tin, 7.5 cm/3 inch deep. Line the base with greaseproof (wax) paper and grease the paper. Process the biscuits (crackers) and hazelnuts in a food processor until fine crumbs form. Pour in the butter and cinnamon. Process just until blended. Using the back of a spoon, press on to the base and to within 1 cm/½ inch of the top of the tin. Bake for 5–7 minutes, until just set. Put the tin on a wire rack to cool. Lower the oven temperature to 150°C/300°F/Gas 2.

2 To prepare the filling, in a small saucepan over a low heat stir together the white chocolate and cream until smooth. Leave to cool. In a large bowl beat the cream cheese and sugar until smooth. Add the eggs one at a time, beating well after each addition. Slowly beat in the white chocolate mixture and liqueur or vanilla essence (extract). Pour into the baked crust. Place the tin on a baking (cookie) sheet. Bake for 45–55 minutes, or until the edge of the cake is firm but the centre slightly soft. Do not allow to brown. Place on a wire rack. Increase the oven temperature to 200°C/400°F/Gas 6.

3 To prepare the topping, in a small bowl whisk together the sour cream, sugar and liqueur or vanilla. Pour over the cheesecake, spreading evenly, and return to the oven. Bake for 5–7 minutes. Turn off the oven, but do not open the door for 1 hour.

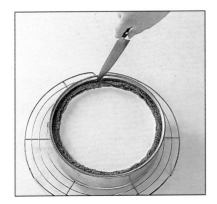

4 Place the tin on a wire rack to cool to room temperature. Run a knife around the edge of the cake to separate it from the side; this helps prevent cracking. Cool then chill, loosely covered, overnight. To serve, remove the side of the springform tin. Place a large palette knife (metal spatula) between the base of the tin and the lining paper and slide the cake and paper base on to a serving plate. Decorate top of cake with chocolate curls and dust lightly with cocoa.

APRICOT BRANDY-SNAP ROULADE

A magnificent combination of soft and crisp textures, this cake looks impressive and is easy to prepare.

INGREDIENTS

Serves 6–8
4 size 3 eggs, separated
½ tbsp fresh orange juice
115 g/4 oz/½ cup caster
(superfine) sugar
175 g/6 oz/1½ cups ground almonds
4 brandy snap biscuits (cookies),
crushed, to decorate

FOR THE FILLING

150 g/5 oz can apricots, drained
300 ml/½ pint/1¼ cups double
(heavy) cream
25 g/1 oz/4 tbsp icing (confectioner's)
sugar

STORING

This cake is not suitable for storing.

1 Preheat the oven to 190°C/375°F/ Gas 5. Grease a 33 x 23 cm/ 13 x 9 inch Swiss roll tin (jelly roll pan), line with greaseproof (wax) paper and grease the paper. Place the egg yolks, orange juice and sugar in a bowl and beat with an electric mixer for 10 minutes until thick and pale. Fold in the ground almonds.

3 To make the filling, purée the apricots in a blender or food processor. Place the cream and icing (confectioner's) sugar in a mixing bowl and whip until it holds soft peaks. Fold in the apricot purée.

2 Whisk the egg whites until they hold stiff peaks and fold into the almond mixture. Transfer to the prepared tin and smooth the surface. Bake in the centre of the oven for about 20 minutes or until a skewer inserted into the centre comes out clean. Leave to cool in the tin, covered with a clean, just-damp dish towel.

4 Spread out the crushed brandy snaps on a sheet of greaseproof paper. Spread about one-third of the cream mixture over the cake, then invert it on to the crushed brandy snaps. Peel away the lining paper. Use the remaining cream to cover the cake. Using the greaseproof paper as a guide, tightly roll up the roulade from a short end. Transfer to a serving dish, sticking on any remaining pieces of brandy snaps.

Fresh Fruit Genoese

*This Italian classic, "Genovese con Panne e Frutta", can be made with
any type of soft fresh fruit.*

Ingredients

Serves 8–10
For the Sponge
*175 g/6 oz/1½ cups plain (all-purpose)
flour, sifted
pinch of salt
4 size 3 eggs
115 g/4 oz/½ cup caster
(superfine) sugar
6 tbsp orange-flavoured liqueur*

For the Filling and Topping
*600 ml/1 pint/2½ cups double
(heavy) cream
4 tbsp vanilla sugar
450 g/1 lb fresh soft fruit, such as
raspberries, blueberries, cherries, etc.
150 g/5 oz/1¼ cups shelled pistachios,
finely chopped
4 tbsp apricot preserve, warmed and
sieved, to glaze*

Storing
This cake is not suitable for storing.

1 Preheat the oven to 180°C/350°F/
Gas 4. Grease a 21 cm/8½ inch
round springform cake tin, line the
base with greaseproof (wax) paper
and grease the paper. Sift the flour
and salt together three times, then set
aside. Place the eggs and sugar in a
mixing bowl and beat with an
electric mixer for about 10 minutes
or until thick and pale.

3 Cut the cake horizontally into
two layers, and place the base
layer on a serving plate. Sprinkle the
orange-flavoured liqueur over both
layers. Place the double (heavy)
cream and vanilla sugar in a mixing
bowl and beat with an electric mixer
until it holds soft peaks.

2 Sift the reserved flour mixture
into the mixing bowl, then fold
in very gently. Transfer the cake
mixture to the prepared tin. Bake in
the centre of the oven for 30–35
minutes or until a skewer inserted
into the centre of the cake comes out
clean. Leave the cake in the tin for
about 5 minutes, then turn out on to
a wire rack, peel off the lining paper
and leave to cool completely.

4 Spread two-thirds of the cream
over the base layer of cake and
top with half the fruit. Place the
second layer of cake on top and
spread the remaining cream over the
top and sides. Using a palette knife
(metal spatula), lightly press the
chopped nuts evenly around the
sides. Arrange the remaining fresh
fruit on top and brush lightly with
the apricot jam.

CHOCOLATE CAPPUCCINO CAKE

*If desired the cake can be left whole and rolled roulade-style, or baked in
2 x 23 cm/9 inch tins for a round cake.*

INGREDIENTS

SERVES 8–10
175 g/6 oz plain (semi-sweet)
chocolate, chopped
2 tsp instant espresso powder
dissolved in 3 tbsp boiling water
6 size 3 eggs, separated
150 g/5 oz/¾ cup granulated sugar
pinch of cream of tartar
unsweetened cocoa powder, for sifting
chocolate-coated coffee beans,
to decorate

FOR THE COFFEE CREAM FILLING
175 ml/6 fl oz/¾ cup whipping cream
25 g/1 oz/2 tbsp granulated sugar
225 g/8 oz/1 cup mascarpone or cream
cheese, softened
2 tbsp coffee-flavoured liqueur
25 g/1 oz plain (semi-sweet) chocolate,
grated

FOR THE COFFEE BUTTERCREAM
4 egg yolks, at room temperature
70 ml/2½ fl oz/¼ cup light golden
syrup (corn syrup)
50 g/2 oz/¼ cup granulated sugar
225 g/8 oz/1 cup unsalted (sweet)
butter, diced and softened
1 tbsp instant espresso powder
dissolved in 1–2 tsp boiling water
15–30 ml/1–2 tbsp coffee-flavoured
liqueur

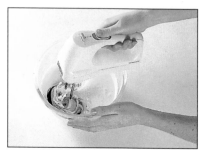

1 Preheat the oven to 180°C/350°F/
Gas 4. Grease a 40 x 27 cm/
15½ x 10½ inch baking (cookie)
sheet. Line with non-stick baking
paper (baking parchment), leaving a
5 cm/2 inch overhang on each narrow
end. Grease the paper. In a double
boiler, over a low heat, heat the
chocolate and coffee liquid until they
are melted and smooth, stirring
frequently. Set aside. In a bowl whisk
the egg yolks and sugar with an
electric mixer until thick and pale.
Gently stir in the chocolate mixture
until evenly blended.

2 In a large bowl beat the egg
whites and cream of tartar until
stiff. Stir a spoonful of whites into
the chocolate mixture to lighten it,
then fold in the rest. Pour the batter
into the prepared tin, spreading into
the corners. Bake for 12–15 minutes
until the top springs back when
touched lightly with a fingertip.
Sprinkle a clean dish towel with
cocoa powder, and then cover and
turn the cake out on to it. Peel off
the paper and cool.

3 To prepare the coffee cream
filling, whip the cream and
sugar in a large bowl until soft peaks
form. In another bowl, beat the
mascarpone or cream cheese and
coffee-flavoured liqueur until smooth.
Stir in the grated chocolate and fold
in the whipped cream. Cover and
chill until needed.

4 To prepare the buttercream, in a bowl with an electric mixer beat the yolks until thick and pale. In a saucepan over a medium heat, cook the syrup and sugar until boiling, stirring constantly. Slowly pour the hot syrup over the beaten yolks in a slow stream, beating continuously. Continue beating until the mixture is cool. Gradually beat in the butter until the mixture is smooth. Beat in the coffee and liqueur. Chill until thick enough to spread.

5 To assemble the cake, with a serrated knife, trim the edges of the cake. Cut the cake crossways into three equal strips. Place one cake strip on a plate and spread with half the coffee cream filling. Cover with a second cake strip and the remaining filling. Top with the remaining cake strip. Spoon about one-third of the coffee buttercream into a small piping bag fitted with a small star nozzle. Then spread the remaining buttercream on the top and sides of the cake. Pipe decoratively on the top and edges of the cake and decorate with chocolate-coated coffee beans.

STRAWBERRY CREAM GATEAU

Fresh raspberries also work well for this recipe.

INGREDIENTS

SERVES 8–10
2 egg yolks
4 size 3 eggs
finely grated rind of 1 lemon
115 g/4 oz/½ cup caster
(superfine) sugar
115 g/4 oz/1 cup plain (all-purpose)
flour, sifted
115 g/4 oz/½ cup butter, melted

FOR THE STRAWBERRY CREAM

225 g/8 oz/1½ cups fresh strawberries,
washed, dried and hulled
300 ml/½ pint/1¼ cups double (heavy)
cream
50 g/2 oz/½ cup icing (confectioner's)
sugar
1 tbsp strawberry liqueur or Kirsch

STORING

This cake can be kept for up to 2 days
in the refrigerator.

1 Preheat the oven to 150°C/300°F/ Gas 2. Grease a deep 20 cm/ 8 inch round cake tin, line the base with greaseproof (wax) paper and grease the paper. Place the egg yolks, eggs, lemon rind and sugar in a mixing bowl and beat with an electric mixer for about 10 minutes or until thick and pale. Add the flour and melted butter. Whisk for a further minute, then transfer to the prepared cake tin.

2 Bake in the centre of the oven for 30–35 minutes or until a skewer inserted into the centre of the cake comes out clean. Turn out on to a wire rack, peel off the lining paper and leave to cool completely.

3 To make the strawberry cream, place all but one of the strawberries in a food processor or blender and purée until smooth. Place the double (heavy) cream in a mixing bowl and whisk until it holds soft peaks. Fold the purée into the cream with the icing (confectioner's) sugar and liqueur or Kirsch.

4 Place the cooled cake on a plate and spread the strawberry cream evenly over the top and the sides, making swirls to create an attractive finish. Slice the reserved strawberry and use to decorate the cake top.

BAKED CHEESECAKE WITH FRESH FRUITS

A rich, creamy cheesecake, baked on a sweet biscuit (graham cracker) base. It is topped with a selection of exotic fresh fruits; vary the decoration to suit the season.

INGREDIENTS

SERVES 12

175 g/6 oz/1¼ cups crushed digestive
biscuits (graham crackers)
50 g/2 oz/¼ cup unsalted (sweet)
butter, melted
450 g/1 lb curd cheese (farmer's-style
cottage cheese)
150 ml/¼ pint/⅔ cup sour cream
115 g/4 oz/½ cup caster
(superfine) sugar
3 size 3 eggs, separated
grated rind 1 lemon
2 tbsp Marsala
½ tsp almond essence (extract)
50 g/2 oz/½ cup ground almonds
50 g/2 oz/scant ½ cup sultanas
(golden raisins)

FOR THE TOPPING

450 g/1 lb prepared mixed fruits – figs,
cherries, peaches, strawberries, hulled,
halved and stoned (pitted),
as necessary

STORING

*This cake can be kept in the
refrigerator in an airtight container for
up to 3 days.*

1 Preheat the oven to 180°C/350°F/ Gas 4. Grease a 25 cm/10 inch round springform tin. Line the side of the tin with non-stick baking paper (baking parchment).

3 Whisk the egg whites until stiff and then fold into the creamed mixture, with both the remaining ingredients, until evenly combined. Pour over the chilled biscuit base (crust) and bake for 45 minutes, until risen and just set in the centre.

2 Mix the biscuits (graham crackers) with the butter until well combined and press into the base of the prepared tin. Smooth the surface with a metal spoon and chill for 20 minutes. Meanwhile prepare the cake mixture. Beat the cheese, cream, sugar, egg yolks, lemon rind, Marsala and almond essence (extract) together until smooth and creamy.

4 Remove from the oven and leave in the tin in a warm, draught-free place, until completely cold. Remove the side of the tin and peel off the lining paper. Chill for 1 hour before decorating with the prepared fruits, just before serving.

SIMNEL CAKE

A traditional cake for Easter.

INGREDIENTS

SERVES 10–12
225 g/8 oz/1 cup butter, softened
225 g/8 oz/1 cup caster
(superfine) sugar
4 size 3 eggs, beaten
550 g/1¼ lb/3 cups mixed dried fruit
115 g/4 oz/½ cup glacé (candied)
cherries
3 tbsp sherry (optional)
280 g/10 oz/2½ cups plain
(all-purpose) flour, sifted
3 tsp mixed spice (apple pie spice)
1 tsp baking powder
675 g/1½ lb yellow marzipan
1 tbsp sieved (strained) apricot jam
1 egg yolk, beaten
ribbons and sugared eggs, to decorate

STORING

This cake can be kept for up to 2
weeks in an airtight container.

1 Preheat the oven to 160°C/325°F/
Gas 3. Lightly grease a deep
20 cm/8 inch round cake tin, then
carefully line with a double thickness
of greaseproof (wax) paper and
grease the paper. Place the softened
butter and caster (superfine) sugar in
a bowl and beat with an electric
mixer until light and fluffy. Gradually
beat in the eggs, beating well after
each addition. Stir in the dried fruit,
glacé (candied) cherries and sherry,
if using. Sift together the plain
(all-purpose) flour, mixed spice
(apple pie spice) and baking powder,
then fold into the cake mixture. Set
aside until needed.

2 Cut off half of the marzipan and
roll it out on a work surface
that has been lightly dusted with
icing (confectioner's) sugar to a
round measuring 20 cm/8 inch.
Spoon half of the cake mixture into
the prepared tin and smooth the
surface with the back of a spoon.
Place the marzipan round on top,
then add the other half of the cake
mixture and smooth the surface.

4 Roll out the other half of the
marzipan to a round to fit on
top of the cake. Brush the top of the
cake with the jam and position the
marzipan on top. Flute the edges of
the marzipan and make a decorative
pattern on top with a fork. Brush
with egg yolk. Put the cake on a
baking (cookie) sheet and place
under a grill (broiler) for 5 minutes
or until the top is lightly browned.
Leave the cake to cool completely
before decorating with ribbons
and sugared eggs.

3 Bake in the centre of the oven
for about 2½ hours or until
golden and springy to the touch.
Leave the cake in the tin for about
15 minutes, then turn out on to a
wire rack, peel off the lining paper
and leave to cool completely.

NUT AND CANDIED FRUIT RING

*The cake can be made 2–3 weeks before Christmas. Store it
in a tin in a cool place until needed.*

INGREDIENTS

SERVES 10–12
*115 g/4 oz/½ cup glacé (candied)
cherries, quartered*
*115 g/4 oz/generous ¾ cup raisins or
sultanas (golden raisins)*
*115 g/4 oz/½ cup dried apricots,
quartered*
*115 g/4 oz dried prunes, stoned
(pitted) and quartered*
*115 g/4 oz/⅔ cup stoned (pitted) and
chopped dates*
4 tbsp rum, brandy or sherry
115 g/4 oz/½ cup butter
*115 g/4 oz/½ cup soft dark brown
sugar*
½ tsp ground cinnamon
*½ tsp mixed spice
(apple pie spice)*
2 size 3 eggs, beaten
50 g/2 oz/½ cup ground almonds
*115 g/4 oz/1 cup coarsely chopped
walnuts*
225 g/8 oz/2 cups self-raising flour

FOR THE TOPPING
2 tbsp rum, brandy or sherry
4 tbsp apricot jam
whole blanched almonds, split
3 glacé (candied) cherries, halved
a few strips of angelica

STORING
*This cake will keep for 2–3 weeks in
an airtight container.*

1 The day before you bake the
cake, soak all the dried fruit in
the rum, brandy or sherry. Cover
and leave overnight. Grease a 23 cm/
9 inch ring tin (ring mold), with a
1.5 litre/2½ pint/6¼ cup capacity.

2 Preheat the oven to 160°C/325°F/
Gas 3. In a bowl, beat the butter,
sugar and spices together until light
and fluffy. Beat in the eggs, and fold
in the soaked fruits. Mix in the
almonds, walnuts and flour.

3 Spoon the mixture into the
prepared cake tin, level the top
and bake for 1½– 2 hours or until a
skewer inserted into the centre comes
out clean. Leave to cool in the tin
for 30 minutes then turn out on to a
wire rack to cool completely. Brush
with the rum, brandy or sherry.

4 Gently heat the apricot jam in a
small pan. Sieve (strain) the jam.
Brush the glaze over the top of the
cake. Decorate with the nuts and
fruit and brush them liberally with
more apricot glaze, which must be
hot, or the decoration will lift off
while you are brushing on the jam.

MOIST AND RICH CHRISTMAS CAKE

The cake can be made 4–6 weeks before Christmas. During this time,
pierce the cake with a fine skewer and spoon over 2–3 tbsp brandy.

INGREDIENTS

MAKES 1 CAKE
225 g/8 oz/generous 1½ cups sultanas
(golden raisins)
225 g/8 oz/1 cup currants
225 g/8 oz/generous 1½ cups raisins
115 g/4 oz dried prunes, stoned
(pitted) and chopped
50 g/2 oz glacé (candied) cherries,
halved
50 g/2 oz/¾ cup mixed (candied) peel,
chopped
3 tbsp brandy or sherry
225 g/8 oz/2 cups plain (all-purpose)
flour
pinch of salt
½ tsp ground cinnamon
½ tsp grated nutmeg
1 tbsp cocoa powder
225 g/8 oz/1 cup butter
225 g/8 oz/1 generous cup soft dark
brown sugar
4 size 1 eggs
finely grated rind of 1 orange or
lemon
50 g/2 oz/½ cup ground almonds
50 g/2 oz/½ cup chopped almonds

TO DECORATE
4 tbsp apricot jam
25 cm/10 in round cake board
450 g/1 lb marzipan
450 g/1 lb white fondant icing
225 g/8 oz royal icing
1.5 m/1½ yd ribbon

1 The day before baking the cake, put all the fruit to soak in the brandy or sherry. Cover and leave overnight. Grease a 20 cm/8 inch deep round cake tin and line it with a double thickness of greaseproof (wax) paper.

2 The next day, preheat the oven to 160°C/325°F/Gas 3. Sift together the flour, salt, spices and cocoa powder. Beat the butter and sugar together until light and fluffy and beat in the eggs gradually. Mix in the orange or lemon rind, the ground and chopped almonds, dried fruits (with any liquid) and the flour mixture. Spoon into the prepared cake tin and level the top. Bake for 3 hours, or until a skewer inserted into the centre comes out clean.

3 Transfer the cake tin to a wire rack and leave to cool for an hour. Carefully turn the cake out on to the wire rack, but leave the paper on if the cake is to be stored, as it will help to keep it moist. Warm then sieve (strain) the apricot jam to make a glaze. Remove the paper from the cake, place on a cake board and brush with apricot glaze. Cover the cake with marzipan and then fondant icing. Pipe a border around the base of the cake with royal icing. Tie a ribbon around the sides. Roll out any fondant icing trimmings and stamp out 12 small holly leaves with a cutter. Make one bell motif with a biscuit cutter, dusted first with sifted icing (confectioner's) sugar. Roll 36 small balls for the holly berries. Leave on greaseproof (wax) paper to dry for 24 hours. Then use to decorate the cake attaching them with a little royal icing.

PASSION CAKE

The icing thickens quickly as it cools and will become difficult to spread, so have the cake on a serving plate and a palette knife (metal spatula) ready to spread the icing.

INGREDIENTS

SERVES 8

150 g/5 oz/⅔ cup butter
200 g/7 oz/scant 1 cup soft light
brown sugar
2 size 3 eggs, beaten
175 g/6 oz carrots, finely grated
finely grated rind of 1 orange
large pinch of salt
1 tsp ground cinnamon
½ tsp grated nutmeg
200 g/7 oz/1¼ cups self-raising flour
1 tsp baking powder
115 g/4 oz/generous ¾ cup raisins
50 g/2 oz/½ cup chopped walnuts
2 tbsp milk

FOR THE ICING

450 g/1 lb/2¼ cups granulated sugar
150 ml/¼ pint/⅔ cup water
pinch of cream of tartar
2 egg whites

STORING

This cake will keep for up to 4 days, covered, in a cool place.

1 Preheat the oven to 190°C/375°F/ Gas 5. Grease two 20 cm/8 inch sandwich tins, then line the bases with greaseproof (wax) paper and grease the paper.

3 Spoon the mixture into the prepared cake tins and bake for 25–30 minutes, or until the cakes are firm to the touch. Leave the cakes to cool in the tins for 5 minutes. Then turn out on to a wire rack and leave to cool completely.

2 In a bowl, beat together the butter and sugar until pale and fluffy. Beat in the eggs gradually and then stir in all the remaining ingredients to make a mixture with a soft dropping consistency.

4 For the icing, put the sugar and water in a pan and heat very gently to dissolve the sugar. (Swirl the pan to mix the sugar, do not stir it with a spoon.) Add the cream of tartar and bring to the boil. Boil until the syrup reaches 115°C/240°F on a sugar thermometer or the soft ball stage. Quickly dip the base of the pan in cold water. Whisk the egg whites until they are stiff and pour the syrup on to them, whisking all the time. Continue whisking until the icing loses its satiny appearance and holds its shape. Quickly sandwich the cakes with some of the icing and spread the rest over the top and side of the cake.

CHOCOLATE CHRISTMAS LOG

Begin preparations for this cake at least 1 day ahead as although it is easy to prepare it has several components.

INGREDIENTS

SERVES 12–14
5 size 3 eggs, separated
20 g/¾ oz/3 tbsp unsweetened cocoa powder, plus extra for dusting
115 g/4 oz/1 cup icing (confectioner's) sugar
¼ tsp cream of tartar

FOR THE CHOCOLATE GANACHE FROSTING
300 ml/½ pint/1¼ cups double (heavy) or whipping cream
350 g/12 oz bittersweet chocolate, chopped
2 tbsp brandy or chocolate-flavour liqueur

FOR THE CRANBERRY SAUCE
450 g/1 lb fresh or frozen cranberries, rinsed and picked over
280 g/10 oz/1 cup seedless raspberry preserve, melted
90 g/3½ oz/½ cup granulated sugar, or to taste

FOR THE WHITE CHOCOLATE CREAM FILLING
200 g/7 oz fine quality white chocolate, chopped
475 ml/16 fl oz/2 cups double (heavy) cream
2 tbsp brandy or chocolate-flavour liqueur (optional)

1 To make the ganache frosting, in a saucepan over a medium heat, bring the cream to the boil. Remove from the heat and add the chocolate all at once, stirring constantly until smooth. Stir in the liqueur, if using, then strain into a bowl and cool. Chill until needed.

3 For the cake, preheat the oven to 200°C/400°F/Gas 6. Grease a 39 x 26 cm/15½ x 10½ inch Swiss roll tin (jelly roll pan), line with non-stick baking paper (baking parchment), overlapping the edge by 2.5 cm/1 inch. Whisk the egg yolks until thick and creamy. Whisk in the cocoa and half the sugar. In a large bowl whisk the egg whites until frothy. Add the cream of tartar and whisk until soft peaks form. Add the remaining sugar, 2 tbsp at a time, whisking well after each addition, until stiff and glossy. Fold the yolk mixture into the whites.

2 To make the sauce, in a food processor, process the cranberries until liquid. Press through a sieve (strainer) into a bowl, discarding the pulp. Stir in the raspberry preserve and sugar to taste. If sauce is too thick, add a little water.

4 Spread the batter in the prepared tin and bake for 15–20 minutes. Lay a clean dish towel on a work surface and cover with non-stick baking paper; dust with cocoa or sugar. Immediately turn the cake out on to the paper. Peel off the lining paper. Trim the edges and, starting from one narrow end, roll up the cake together with the paper and towel. Leave to cool.

5 To make the filling, in a saucepan gently heat the white chocolate with 120 ml/4 fl oz/½ cup cream until melted, stirring frequently. Strain into a bowl and cool. Whisk the remaining cream and brandy until soft peaks form. Stir a spoonful of cream into the white chocolate mixture to lighten it, then fold in remaining cream. Unroll the cake and spread with chocolate cream. Starting from the same end, re-roll the cake without the paper. Cut off one-quarter at an angle. Place against the long piece to resemble a branch.

6 Allow the frosting to soften at room temperature. With an electric mixer, beat the ganache until light in colour and texture, about 30–45 seconds. It should be a soft spreading consistency; do not over-beat as it will become stiff and grainy. Using a palette knife (metal spatula), spread the ganache over the cake. Using a fork, mark to resemble tree bark. Then dust with icing (confectioner's) sugar and serve with the cranberry sauce.

PANFORTE

This rich, spicy nougat-type cake is a speciality of Siena in Italy,
where it is traditionally baked at Christmas.

INGREDIENTS

SERVES 8

280 g/10 oz/2 cups mixed (candied)
exotic peel, to include: papaya,
pineapple, orange, lemon and citron
115 g/4 oz/1 cup unblanched almonds
50 g/2 oz/½ cup walnut halves
50 g/2 oz/½ cup plain
(all-purpose) flour
1 tsp ground cinnamon
¼ tsp each grated nutmeg, ground
cloves and ground coriander
175 g/6 oz/¾ cup caster (superfine)
sugar
4 tbsp water
icing (confectioner's) sugar,
to decorate

STORING

This cake will keep well for several
weeks in an airtight container.

1 Preheat the oven to 180°C/350°F/
Gas 4. Grease a 20 cm/8 inch
round loose-based tin and line the
base with a circle of rice paper.
Combine the mixed (candied) peel
and almonds and walnuts in a bowl.
Sift in the flour and all the spices
and mix well. Heat the sugar and
water in a small pan, stirring until
the sugar is completely dissolved.
Increase the heat and boil until the
mixture reaches 115°C/220°F on a
sugar thermometer, or until it reaches
the thread stage.

2 Remove from the heat and pour
on to the fruit mixture, stirring
with a wooden spoon until well-
coated. Transfer to the prepared tin,
pressing out with the back of a metal
spoon. Bake in the centre of the oven
for 25–30 minutes, until the mixture
is bubbling. Remove from the oven
and cool in the tin for 5 minutes.

3 With a lightly oiled palette knife
(metal spatula) work around the
edge of the cake, to loosen and
remove from the tin leaving the base
in place. Leave until cold.

4 Remove the panforte from
the base and decorate with a
generous dusting of icing
(confectioner's) sugar.

INDEX